China's Special Gifts to the World

by Linda Yoshizawa

illustrated by Burgundy Beam

Scott Foresman
is an imprint of

Glenview, Illinois • Boston, Massachusetts • Chandler, Arizona
Upper Saddle River, New Jersey

Illustrations by Burgundy Beam

ISBN 13: 978-0-328-51424-3
ISBN 10:   0-328-51424-1

9 10 11 12 V0FL 16 15 14 13

TABLE OF CONTENTS

CHAPTER 1   4
The Wonders of Asia

CHAPTER 2   5
The Language of China

CHAPTER 3   7
Language as Art

CHAPTER 4   9
The Poet Li Po

CHAPTER 5   11
The Calligrapher's Tools

CHAPTER 6   17
Learning Calligraphy

Now Try This   20

Glossary   22

Chapter 1

The Wonders of Asia

In the late 1200s, Marco Polo, the young son of a trader, traveled to the Far East with his father. For seventeen years, he journeyed throughout China and the Far East.

On his journeys, Marco Polo saw many of the wonders of Asia. He saw precious jewels, gold-paved streets, beautiful silk clothing in bright colors, and he tasted all kinds of wonderful spices. He also discovered the beautiful Chinese language.

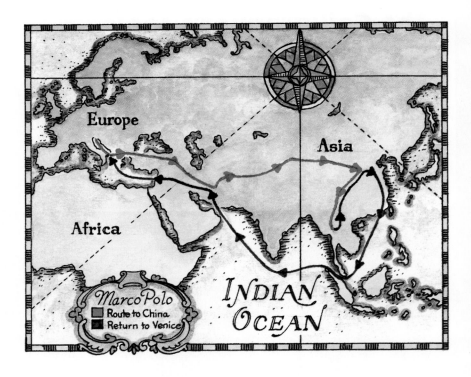

Chapter 2
The Language of China

China's towering mountains and huge deserts kept it isolated from Europe for many years. During those years, Chinese civilization **flourished.** The ancient Chinese knew how to make paper several centuries before the Europeans. They also knew how to print with movable type. The ancient Chinese invented gunpowder—which they used to make rockets and bombs—and they invented a system of writing.

By the third century A.D., the Chinese understood how magnets worked. They used magnets to invent a compass.

Today, China is one of the largest and most populated countries in the world. With so much land and so many people, it's not surprising that the country is so **diverse.** People in different parts of China even speak different **dialects,** or versions, of the Chinese language.

No matter what dialect they speak, **literate** Chinese can read the same written language, because the language is written in pictures called characters instead of letters. Each picture stands for a word or an idea. The written language has kept the people united.

心 heart   魚 fish

金 gold   識 knowledge

面 face   鼻 nose

Chinese characters

Chapter 3
Language as Art

Most languages change over time. The written language of China has not changed much over the years, though, and modern Chinese scholars can easily read ancient poetry just as it was first written. No **translation** is needed!

Literature has always been an important part of Chinese culture, so it is a good thing that the literature of the past is easy for people in China to read today.

In China, literature is important for its history, ideas, and the beautiful way it is written. Chinese writing is also known as calligraphy.

Chinese calligraphers do not use an alphabet to write individual letters that form words as we do. Instead, they paint a character. Each character is a little picture that stands for one object or idea.

Each small character is a work of art in itself. Scholars study and practice for many years to learn how to make each character. Then, they practice drawing them in their own individual styles.

Even people who do not read Chinese enjoy looking at the characters drawn by calligraphers. Examples of the art of calligraphy appear in museums all around the world. You could also find examples of this art hanging on the walls in people's homes. To many art lovers, calligraphy is a much loved and treasured form of fine art.

A Chinese poem

Chapter 4
The Poet Li Po

From ancient to modern times, China has had many famous poets, novelists, and essay writers. One of the best known is the poet Li Po.

Li Po lived from 701 to 762, during the Tang Dynasty, a period in Chinese history when all the arts flourished. He wrote about everyday ideas. His writing was happy and light, celebrating the delights of life.

Li Po's favorite subjects were nature, friends, and the joy of spending time alone. Although he had a family and spent time living at the emperor's court, he often took time off for "wandering." Perhaps his journeys gave him the **inspiration** for his poems.

Li Po won lasting fame as a poet. Sadly, though, he failed to achieve one of his life's goals: the emperor never gave him an official title. Disappointed, he joined a military **expedition.** The emperor thought the purpose of the expedition was to create a new dynasty, and he became angry. He had the leader of the expedition killed and he jailed Li Po.

Chapter 5
The Calligrapher's Tools

Ancient calligraphers used special tools for writing that they referred to as "the four treasures." One treasure was their collection of special brushes. They also needed ink sticks and ink stones to make ink. The fourth treasure was fine paper.

夜思

床前明月光
疑是地上霜
舉頭望明月
低頭思故鄉

You ask me why I dwell in the green mountain,
I smile and make no reply for my heart is free of care.
As the peach-blossom flows downstream and is gone into the unknown,
I have a world apart that is not among men.

The first calligraphy brushes were made at least 4000 years ago. Modern brushes have not changed much. The **bristles** are still made from animal hair attached to bamboo reeds.

Brushes come in different sizes, and the bristles have different textures too. Some are soft, and some are stiff, while others have a mixture of soft and stiff bristles.

Brush makers use many different kinds of animal hair. They use hair from goats, wolves, deer, sheep, and foxes.

Ancient calligraphers did not buy ink in a bottle. They made their own ink, using an ink stick and an ink stone.

Like other traditional calligraphy materials, ink sticks have been used for thousands of years. The basic **ingredient** in an ink stick is soot. Soot is the black substance in smoke that comes after you burn something. Some ink sticks use soot from burned pine trees or oil.

The soot is collected and mixed with other ingredients that hold it together. Then the sticks are formed and decorated.

Good ink sticks can last as long ten years. Surprisingly, the best way to determine an ink stick's quality is to tap it and listen to the sound. The sound should be clear and sharp, not **muffled.**

13

An ink stick is not like chalk; it is too hard and solid to write with. After calligraphers choose the best ink stick, they need to turn it into ink. To do this, they need an ink stone.

Calligraphers use ink stones to grind tiny flakes off the ink stick. Then they mix the flakes with water to make a liquid.

To make ink, artists start by putting a little cool water on the stone. Water that has a small amount of salt works best. Then they rub the stick in the water. Once they have made a thick liquid, they add a little more water and rub some more. They keep working until the ink is just they way they want it.

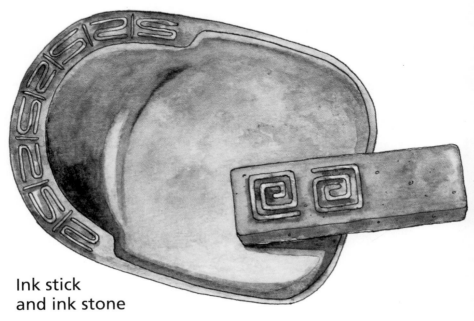

Ink stick
and ink stone

Tips for Making Calligraphy Ink

1. Use the best ink stick you can find.

2. Use water that has a little bit of salt. If you cannot use saltwater, use well water, tap water, or bottled distilled water.

3. Start with a small amount of water.

4. Press the ink stick against the stone and rub lightly in circles.

5. Grind all the ink for one project at the same time. It is hard to make two batches of ink that are exactly the same color.

6. Don't make the ink too thick. Thick ink makes brush bristles stick together.

7. Don't make the ink too thin. Thin ink may go right through the paper.

8. Use the ink right away.

Calligraphers can paint their beautiful characters on any kind of surface. Some artists draw on silk; most use special paper.

Artists who want their work to last a long time use a special kind of paper called Xuan paper. Some artwork made on Xuan paper has lasted a thousand years. Xuan paper does not tear easily and will not be damaged by insects. Even if the paper gets wet, the artwork will not be destroyed.

Chapter 6
Learning Calligraphy

Calligraphy is not easy to learn. The Chinese written language has about 50,000 characters. About 7,000 characters are commonly used. Calligraphers spend years studying them.

Calligraphy students begin by learning basic **techniques.** They learn the right way to hold the brush. They learn the correct posture for writing. Then, they learn the basic brushstrokes.

After that, they practice, practice, and practice! One great artist named Wang Xizhi spent lots of time practicing while he was growing up. After each session, he cleaned his brushes in the pond outside his family's home. Some people say he cleaned so many brushes that the whole pond turned black with ink!

Even though China has a new system of alphabetic writing, calligraphy is not a lost art. Many people still use characters to communicate. Character writing is still taught in Chinese schools.

Calligraphy is written in lines from the top of the page to the bottom, beginning on the right side of the page.

Someday character writing may become less common. But many people will still want to learn this ancient and respected art.

Calligraphy is an art form with many traditions. One tradition is about a special way to practice. Practice is done in three stages. The stages are called "mo," "lin," and "xie".

During the "mo" stage, students learn to practice using a brush to make basic strokes. Then students move on to the "lin" stage. In this stage, they copy a model. Students copy the model onto paper filled with squares.

The "xie" stage is the time for students to write on their own. They begin to write their own thoughts.

In the "xie" stage, students also develop their own style. Everyone's handwriting looks a little different, and calligraphy, after all, is an art!

Be a Calligrapher

Try some calligraphy yourself. Since you are a beginner, you won't use special calligraphy tools. Instead, use a simple paint brush with a fine point and some tempera paint. You can paint on regular art paper.

朋	friend
巒	school
狗	dog
日	sun
笑	laugh

1. Gather the materials you'll need.

2. Practice using the inked paint brush to make different kinds of brushstrokes on the paper.

3. Choose a character from the chart to copy.

4. Study the lines in the character.

5. Trace over the lines with your finger and decide how to form the brushstrokes.

6. Practice! Practice! Practice!

Glossary

bristles *n.* the hairs on a brush

dialects *n.* different versions of a particular language

diverse *adj.* different

expedition *n.* a journey with a specific purpose

flourished *v.* steadily grew; expanded

ingredient *n.* one of several substances mixed together to make a new substance

inspiration *n.* something that stimulates a person to be creative

literate *adj.* having the ability to read and write

muffled *adj.* unable to be heard; wrapped with material to deaden the sound

techniques *n.* methods of doing something

translation *n.* message or text changed from one language into a different language